BY VALERIE BODDEN

CREATIVE EDUCATION

Published by Creative Education
P.O. Box 227, Mankato, Minnesota 56002
Creative Education is an imprint of The Creative Company
www.thecreativecompany.us

Design and production by The Design Lab
Art direction by Rita Marshall
Printed in the United States of America

Photographs by Alamy (NASA), Jay Ireland and Georgienne
Bradley/Bradley Ireland Productions, Corbis (David
Ball, Robert Garvey, Paul A. Souders, Penny Tweedie,
Bill Varie, Lawson Wood), Dreamstime (Banol2007,
Goodolga, Ingvars, Mwookie, Sjm1123, Thomasgulla)

Library of Congress Cataloging-in-Publication Data
Bodden, Valerie.
Great Barrier Reef / by Valerie Bodden.
p. cm. — (Big outdoors)
Summary: A fundamental introduction to the Great Barrier Reef,
including the ocean that surrounds it, the creatures that live near
it, and how people have affected its marine environment.
Includes index.
ISBN 978-1-58341-816-1
1. Great Barrier Reef (Qld.)—Juvenile literature.
2. Coral reef ecology—Australia—Great Barrier Reef
(Qld.)—Juvenile literature. I. Title. II. Series.

GB468.89.B63 2010
551.42'409943—dc22   2009004689

First Edition
9 8 7 6 5 4 3 2 1

GREAT BARRIER REE

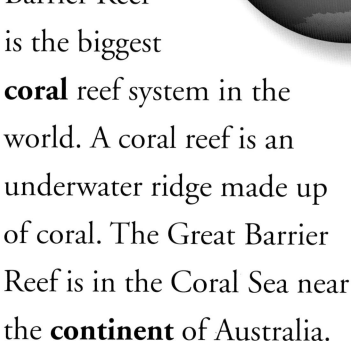

The Great Barrier Reef is the biggest **coral** reef system in the world. A coral reef is an underwater ridge made up of coral. The Great Barrier Reef is in the Coral Sea near the **continent** of Australia.

The Coral Sea is part of the Pacific Ocean near Australia

The Great Barrier Reef is big enough to be spotted from outer space.

Almost 3,000 reefs make up the Great Barrier Reef. The system of reefs is more than 1,400 miles (2,250 km) long. The water near the Great Barrier Reef is clear and warm.

The shallow water around the reef makes it easier to see it

The Great Barrier Reef was made by tiny, tube-shaped animals called coral polyps (*PAH-lips*). Coral polyps live in big groups. They attach themselves to the **skeletons** of other coral. Then they make a skeleton around themselves. When the coral polyps die, their skeletons become part of the coral reef.

Some kinds of coral are soft, but other kinds are as hard as stone

More than 400 different kinds of coral make up the Great Barrier Reef.

The area around the Great Barrier Reef is warm year-round. Sometimes there are big storms called cyclones (*SY-klones*). There are many cities on Australia's **coast** near the Great Barrier Reef.

Port Douglas is a town in Australia that is next to the reef

Colorful fish swim through the Great Barrier Reef. Starfish, eels, and jellyfish live by the reef, too. So do sharks and green sea turtles.

Clownfish (above) and sea turtles (opposite) share the reef's waters

More than 1,500 different kinds of fish swim through the Great Barrier Reef.

BIG OUTDOORS

14

GREAT BARRIER REEF

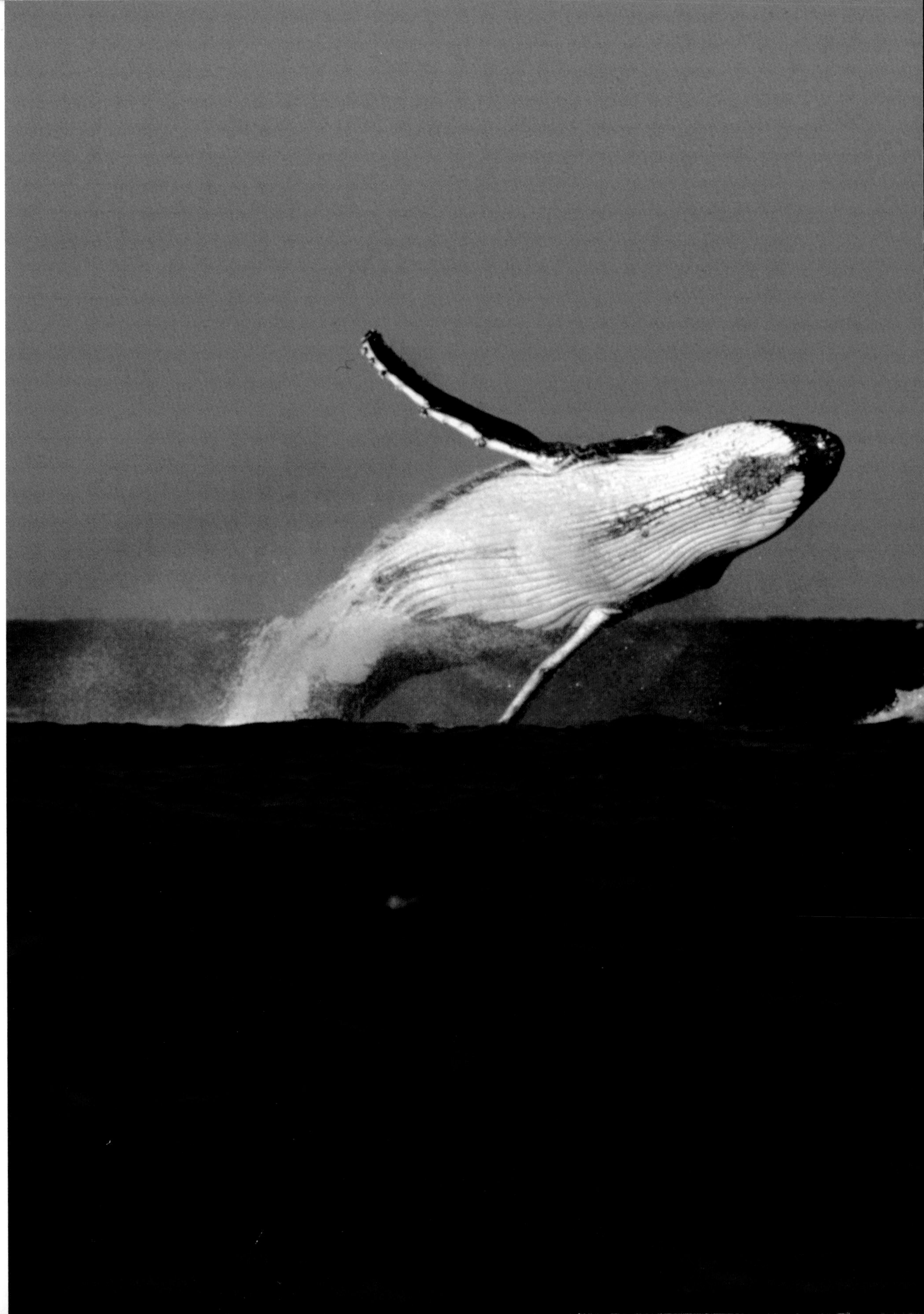

Mangrove trees grow in the water near the Great Barrier Reef. Large birds such as herons and egrets live in the trees. Humpback whales and dolphins swim in the water outside the reef.

Humpback whales (opposite) and egrets (above) live nearby

Australian **Aborigines** (*ab-uh-RIJ-uh-neez*) have lived near the Great Barrier Reef for thousands of years. White people first found the reef almost 250 years ago. They came on a ship that crashed into it. Since then, more than 1,500 ships have sunk on the reef.

Native people (opposite) never wrecked ships (above) on the reef

The crown-of-thorns starfish hurts coral reefs by eating coral polyps.

Today, some people take coral from the Great Barrier Reef. Fishers destroy coral with their nets. **Pollution** hurts the reef. But many people are working hard to protect it.

Fishers sometimes use big nets to catch many fish at once

Every year, millions of people visit the Great Barrier Reef. Some dive in the reef's waters. Others take boat trips. Some people even walk on the reef. Visitors are amazed by this colorful underwater world!

Many people enjoy diving underwater to see coral up-close

If the water they live in gets too hot, coral can lose their bright colors.

Coral can look like tree branches, plates, or even giant brains!

Glossary

Aborigines people who lived in Australia before white people arrived

coast the edge of the land closest to the water

continent one of Earth's seven big pieces of land

coral a hard, stony material made from the skeletons of groups of living animals called coral polyps

pollution things such as chemicals that make the earth, water, or air dirty

skeletons animals' hard outer coverings or the bones inside their bodies

Read More about It

Douglas, Lloyd. *Coral Reef.* New York: Children's Press, 2005.

Dunphy, Madeleine. *Here Is the Coral Reef.* New York: Hyperion Books for Children, 1998.

Index